THE FIRST YEAR AFTER LOSS

The GRIEF *Ladies'* Guide to Everything You Need to Know

Karyn Arnold & Kelly Daugherty
The GRIEF Ladies

ISBN (eBook): 979-8-9956740-0-9

ISBN (paperback): 979-8-9956740-1-6

You Don't Have to Do This Alone

Grief is not meant to be carried in silence and alone. The GRIEF Ladies are here for you, through honest conversations on the podcast, connection with others in our Facebook community, and resources designed to help you move forward with love rather than pain.

Scan the QR code to visit us at www.griefladies.com and find everything you need.

DISCLAIMER

This booklet is intended for educational and informational purposes only. The content is not a substitute for professional mental health treatment, grief counseling, or medical advice. Reading this material does not establish a therapeutic relationship with the authors or with Center for Informed Grief, LLC.

If you are experiencing a mental health crisis, please call or text 988 to reach the Suicide and Crisis Lifeline.

GRIEF Ladies is an educational framework developed by the Center for Informed Grief, LLC. The content in this booklet is not therapy.

DEDICATION

This book is dedicated to the people we've lost. To our friends and family who have known grief. To the people we are honored to work with. And to anyone who picks up this book.

Grief has been our greatest teacher — and the people who have moved through it, our most profound guides. In their honor, we offer these pages as a quiet space to begin. May you find permission to grieve in your own way, the patience to let it take the time it takes, grace for yourself and those around you, and in time — peace.

CONTENTS

BEFORE YOU BEGIN

This booklet isn't going to tell you how to stop grieving. It's going to tell you what to expect while you are.

What's ahead isn't a schedule or a set of stages. It's a map of territory that most people find completely unfamiliar, even people who have experienced loss before. And that's because this loss, this person, this absence - and the first year isn't something you can ever really prepare for. So whatever you are feeling right now (or not feeling), it's all part of it.

The goal for this first year is not to heal, move on, or figure out what comes next. The goal is simply to get through it.

This booklet will help you know what that looks like.

THE EARLIEST DAYS

In the beginning, most people are surprised by how much there is to do. Phone calls, paperwork, arrangements, people coming and going. Food appearing at the door. Texts that need answering. A memorial to plan. Accounts to close, subscriptions to cancel, phone plans to sort out. It is exhausting, and it feels endless, and most of it lands at a time when you are not feeling your most capable, clear, or productive.

What many people find, looking back, is that having something to do gave them just that - something to do. As overloaded as they may feel, the business of early grief gives them somewhere to direct their energy besides the loss itself.

This is also the period most people describe as the fog - where shock and disbelief take over, and it may be hard for them to comprehend that this has *actually* happened. Some people describe feeling like their loved one is just away. Not gone...just somewhere else.

Most people don't realize they were in the fog until it lifts. Besides the things that have to get done, this otherwise isn't the time for big decisions.

Sleep when you can. Eat something. Create new systems and write things down - your memory is not reliable right now, and that's to be expected. If someone offers specific help, let them. Everything else can wait.

WHEN THE FOG LIFTS

The fog doesn't lift all at once. It's more gradual than that, and the timing is different for everyone. For some people, it's a few weeks. For others, it takes longer, especially when the loss was sudden.

Though it has to be said: nothing really prepares you. Even people who watched someone decline for a long time will experience shock when the moment comes.

What's hard about this moment is the timing of it. Just as the fog begins to thin and just as reality starts to settle in a new way, most of the people around you have gone back to their lives.

The calls slow down. The food stops coming. People assume that because some time has passed, you are moving along, too.

And some people will disappoint you. Mostly out of discomfort, or not knowing what to say, but it still hurts, and it is one of the more quietly painful and isolating parts of grief.

Family can be complicated in a particular way. In that case, everyone is *also* grieving, but they are not grieving the same person. Your sibling lost a parent - but so did you, and your relationships with that parent were not the same. Your parent lost a spouse, a loss that looks very different than yours. You may find that family cannot always hold each other's grief. They are too deep in their own. It is worth knowing so you don't spend too much energy looking for support in people who don't have it to give right now.

Sometimes it's a spouse or partner who didn't have the same relationship with the person you lost who may struggle to understand the depth of what you're feeling, or how long it's lasting. They love you, and they want to help, but they are watching from the outside of a grief they can't fully enter.

Often the people who can help most are often outside of it - a grief group, or someone who has been through it themselves. Finding even one person who can simply sit with you in it, without needing it to look any particular way, will make a difference.

What all of this can leave you with is a loneliness you weren't expecting, and a grief that feels harder than people around you seem to think it should be. If you can loosen your grip on how you think this should be going, how you think you should be coping, and how you think other people should or shouldn't be showing up for you, you will be better off.

SIGNS AND SYMPTOMS

Of the many surprises, the changes you see in yourself may be the biggest (or at least the most distressing).

The forgetfulness that goes beyond misplacing your keys. Missing appointments you wrote down. Losing track of a conversation mid-sentence. Reading the same paragraph four times and still not knowing what it said. Having no memory of why you walked into the room.

It can make the ordinary feel impossible. Simple tasks like a load of laundry, a dish in the sink, a phone call that needs returning - things that should take only a few minutes can go undone for days. The motivation, the sense that any of it matters, the energy to even begin, can drain away when you are preoccupied with loss, and when you are attempting to function on diminished sleep.

Many grievers feel like they are going "crazy". Some will even worry that they are developing more serious memory problems or dementia; it can be that disorienting and that frightening.

But ALL of these symptoms are very common - they are also temporary.

Some may wonder: how can these symptoms be temporary when the loss itself is not? It's a fair question. After all, something permanent has happened, so the changes and responses can feel permanent too. But there is a difference between the loss, and the symptoms of carrying loss.

In some ways, your mind is working harder than it ever has. It is processing significant loss, managing pain, absorbing a new reality, and trying to keep up with daily life all at the same time. In the midst of this it is also learning, and adjusting, and reshaping - it doesn't know this life without your person in it.

It will adapt, eventually, and that's when many start to see their symptoms ease. In the meantime, it's all about the management of these symptoms - meeting them with grace, patience, and self-compassion whenever you can.

A NOTE ABOUT TRAUMA

Most losses include some degree of trauma. It helps to think of it like a spectrum, where there can be extremes on either end.

Sometimes it happens with a long illness - the things you saw, heard, smelled, and experienced as you watched someone you love decline. Sometimes it's the phone call, the moment you were told, or your proximity to the event as it happened. Sometimes there's a diagnosis with a quick change and decline, and no time to make any sense of it.

Whatever the circumstances, there are often parts of the experience that feel particularly intrusive, especially in the early days. Not all deaths are peaceful, and those final moments can get stuck on a loop in your mind, replaying in ways you didn't choose and can't easily stop. This can also include images that pop into your head out of nowhere, or thoughts that make it difficult to sleep. It may be the reason it is so hard to tell your grief story without breaking down, or why feelings of anxiety, fear, and uncertainty keep surfacing.

On the other side of intrusion is avoidance - steering clear of certain people, places, conversations, or even thoughts that feel like too much to face. Both are normal responses to an overwhelming experience.

The thing about loss is that we're not "just" processing the death - we're also processing what happened leading up to it. Things you didn't have the "luxury" to have feelings or emotions about, especially if you were a caregiver.

When the thoughts become too intrusive, too disruptive, or if it starts to feel like it's taking over even more than the grief itself, know that additional support, especially trauma-informed support, can make a real difference.

SECONDARY LOSSES

If the primary loss is the loss of our person, then secondary losses can best be described as all the things we lose, now that they are no longer here. The loss of income or financial security. The loss of intimacy and companionship. The loss of the person who handled certain things - the bills, the repairs, the navigating of situations you never had to think about before. The loss of your biggest cheerleader. The loss of the person who knew your history, your inside jokes, the version of you that only they saw. The loss of the person you told all of your big news to, and the person you shared the mundane with.

This is part of why losing one person can feel like losing ten. Because they were never just one person to you. Depending on who they were in your life, they may have been your closest friend, your daily companion, your source of stability, your loudest supporter, the keeper of your shared history. They played roles that no one else played, in ways that no one else knew. And every one of those roles can feel empty in their absence.

This is part of why grief is so hard, and part of why it lasts as long as it does. You are not just mourning a person. You are mourning all the thousands of strings that we tied to them, that feel like they were cut very suddenly and all at once.

Maybe some of these losses are already evident. Maybe they haven't quite shown up yet. What matters is that having some idea of what to expect can help you recognize them when they come. The widow who finds herself crying while mowing the lawn - it's not about the lawn. It's about her husband, and the fact that he's not here to do it. The adult child who can't make the drive home from work without falling apart, and can't figure out why - it's the reminder that this was always the time they called mom. Secondary losses are specific, and they are yours. And unfortunately, they tend to be mostly invisible to those around you. Part of your work will be continuing to honor all that has been lost - not just the person, but everything that went with them. Especially if you ever question why you are "still" grieving at any point in this journey.

MORE THAN SAD

This tends to be another surprise. Not the sadness, because most people expect to be sad when someone they love has died. It's everything else that comes with it. The anger, the guilt, the regret, the resentment. These aren't things that are also happening while you are grieving - they are grief.

These can be some of the "ugly" emotions of grief - hard to feel, and even harder to say out loud. But they are worth noticing because they can also be what causes a person to become preoccupied - reliving the time leading up to the loss over and over again.

It can be based on decisions that went into a loved one's care. It can be moments in their relationship going back decades. Things that were said or left unsaid. Decisions that were made, and not made.

Guilt is as much a part of grief as sadness, and it serves a purpose even when we can't see what that is. Sometimes it creates a connection, constantly keeping them in our thoughts, even if those thoughts are very painful. Sometimes it's a way of maintaining control, especially at a time when you're feeling especially helpless.

What can be said is this: at some point down the road, it will be up to you to let yourself off the hook. No one can do that for you. But holding onto guilt indefinitely means that your connection to the person you lost becomes defined by bad feelings.

Everyone, in every relationship, is doing the best they can with what they have. That was true then. It is still true now.

That moment of release may not belong to the first year. But knowing it exists, and that it will be yours to claim when you are ready, is worth holding onto.

GRIEF IN THE BODY

Most people are not prepared for how physical grief is.

The exhaustion that sleep doesn't fix. The headaches. Eating too much or too little. Getting sick more easily than usual - grief has a real effect on the immune system, and the body becomes more vulnerable when we are carrying something this heavy. Some people describe feeling sluggish and weighed down. Others notice they are moving more slowly, with less purpose - like their feet are stuck in concrete. Some catch a glimpse of themselves in the mirror and barely recognize who is looking back - puffy from crying, drawn from not sleeping, visibly changed.

Grief can introduce us to the mind-body connection in a way that few other things can. What we carry emotionally shows up physically. The tension in the jaw and shoulders, the way sadness can feel like an actual physical weight - these are not imaginary. And for those carrying trauma alongside their grief, they may find they are more easily startled, hypervigilant, braced for the next thing. The body is grieving, too.

The complicated part is that grief can look like a lot of things physically, and not all of them can be waited out. If you were a caregiver before this loss, you have likely been neglecting your own physical health and needs for some time. It's a good time for a check-up. Grief is real in the body, but not every physical symptom can or should be attributed to it. Some things need attention, and some need urgent attention - chest pain or tightness, for example, should never be left alone. When the body is sending loud signals, listen.

THE YEAR OF FIRSTS

The first year is full of them. Your first birthday without them. Their first birthday without them. The first Thanksgiving, the first winter holidays, and the first anniversary of their death.

Most of these you can see coming, and the lead-up is often its own kind of hard. The dread that builds in the days before, the way a date sits on the calendar like a weight. And then the days after - the rawness that lingers even when the day itself is behind you.

What most people find is that the days they dreaded most are not always the hardest ones. The anticipated dates come with preparation, with people who remember, with some kind of intention.

Then there are the dates that catch people off guard. Not the obvious ones - but the quieter holidays, the ones you didn't think to worry about. No one is reaching out to check on you. There's no preparation, no plan. What people discover is that almost any occasion creates contrast - the difference between life before and life now, the awareness that everyone around you is gathered with their people, going about their lives, while yours looks completely different. That contrast can be surprisingly painful, even on a day you never would have predicted.

But remember it this way. Every occasion that passes in that first year (and beyond) is providing you with information. How did you get through the day? Did you work or stay home? Were you with people or alone? Did you mark it in some way or let it pass quietly? And whatever you did...did it help or didn't it?

Whatever the answers, pay attention to them. These are the clues that can help you navigate and survive the occasions that follow.

TRIGGERS

Some people call them triggers. Some call them reminders. One woman in a grief group called them grenades. However you refer to them, these are the moments when grief is felt most intensely - sharply, suddenly, and often without warning.

In the first year, triggers are EVERYWHERE.

They are the things around your home that belonged to them. The chair they always sat in. Their side of the closet. The coffee cup they used every morning. They are the places around town you went together. They are songs, smells, and handwriting on an old card.

They are specific to you, and to the person you lost, and to the life you shared. No one else will have exactly the same triggers. Some feel significant, and some will feel almost embarrassingly small. But all of them are real, because they are yours.

The unexpected triggers can be the hardest. There is no preparation for a song that comes on in a waiting room, or running into someone you haven't seen since the loss, and having to go through the whole story all over again. An unexpected trigger can set you back for days.

What many people find is that repetition helps. The more you encounter a place, a song, a person, the more you adjust. Slowly. It doesn't happen easily or quickly. But returning to the same grocery store, sitting in the same chair, going back to the same restaurant - what you can count on is that each time is a little different than the last.

Grieving people often say ″I can′t do this." - when what they usually mean is something even truer and harder than that: "I don′t want to". As in, "I don't want to have to do this life, with this grief, without this person in it."

But people do it. And they do get through it, and the ones who have will tell you it rarely looked like strength. It looked like survival mode. One day, and sometimes one hour, at a time. Not trying to solve the whole thing at once...just finding what was manageable today, and doing that.

GRIEF TOUCHES EVERYTHING

Once you've experienced a significant loss, you quickly find there's no place to escape it.

It doesn't stay home when you go out. It doesn't take breaks when you need one. And things that seemingly have nothing to do with the person you lost - your job, an errand, a conversation that goes sideways - can suddenly feel completely overwhelming.

This surprises people. They expect grief to live in the obvious places - and it does. But it also shows up where you least expect it, in moments that seem to have nothing to do with your loss at all. Because you are different now and therefore everything you encounter is filtered through that difference.

Your threshold has changed. Your reserves are lower. Someone who was relatively easy-going, thick-skinned, not easily bothered may find that grief has changed all of that, at least for now. Feelings get hurt more easily. Work feels harder to tolerate. You're irritable, short-tempered.

Right now, you are a water glass filled to the rim and even a single drop can make you spill over.

Sometimes it's the smallest thing that puts you over the edge. Not the big dates, not the obvious triggers - but the gym that's unexpectedly closed, the errand that can't get done, the one thing you were counting on to get you through the day that doesn't come through. To anyone watching, it looks like an overreaction. But it isn't about the gym. It never is. It's about a lower threshold and not being able to keep it together when one more thing goes wrong.

So when something happens, and your reaction feels bigger than the situation deserves, it's worth noting whether grief is at least partially to blame. It usually is.

WHAT "GETTING BETTER" ACTUALLY MEANS

All the time, in groups and personal sessions, grieving people ask...

"Does it get better?"

Not exactly, at least not in the first year (for most), but it does get different.

The intensity shifts. The weight of it changes. And slowly, parts of yourself that went quiet after the loss start to come back. You pick up a book you haven't been able to touch. You laugh at something and mean it. You have a conversation that has nothing to do with grief, and afterward realize you were fully present for it.

But what's important to remember is that getting better does not mean grieving less. You can be getting better and still crying every day. You can be getting better and still miss them with everything you have. You can be getting better and still have days that feel as hard as the very beginning.

Getting better in grief is not a straight line and not a destination. It is the slow process of reconnecting with the parts of yourself that you recognize. Not returning to who you were before - that person has been changed by this, and that is not something to fix. But instead, it may be about finding yourself again, inside this new reality.

Some people will struggle with this. It can feel like "getting better" is a betrayal somehow - of the person they lost, of the grief itself.

But it isn't. And when it begins, you may notice it less as happiness and more as familiarity. A returning trust in yourself. An old interest that doesn't feel as far away as it did. A moment where you made a decision, or handled something, and felt briefly like yourself again.

The grief is still there, it doesn't leave, but you begin to move alongside it, a little more intentionally, a little less like you are simply surviving it.

IT KEEPS CHANGING

Just when you think you've figured out your grief – when you've learned your triggers, found a few things that help, started to recognize your own patterns - it changes. This is one of the more frustrating parts of the first year. And the second. And the time beyond that, too.

But it is also, in its own way, the most important thing to understand about grief. Because it means that how you feel right now is not how you will always feel. The version of grief you are living with today is not permanent. It will shift, and sometimes in ways that catch you off guard. Sometimes so gradually that you won't even notice until you look back. This is not a promise that it gets easier. It is actually something more reliable than that.

It is the simple fact that grief, like everything else, keeps moving.

And the change is not always welcome. You get used to your grief — the crying, the heaviness, the shape of it — and that familiarity becomes its own strange comfort. Then it shifts. The tears stop, or the anger arrives, or something you thought you'd made peace with surfaces again in a new form. The instinct is to interrogate it — *why am I not crying anymore, why do I want to be alone now, does this mean I've moved on, does this mean I haven't?*

Some versions of grief will feel more right than others. One version may feel like it keeps you closer to the person you lost, and when that version changes, it can feel like a second loss. But grief is not a measure of love, and no version of it is more valid than another.

Try instead to stay curious. Not critical, not alarmed — just curious. Follow where your grief goes, and ask what it might need from you in this new form. The shifts will keep coming. And so will your ability to meet them.

AFTER THE FIRST YEAR

If you are still early in your first year, know that this section will be here when you need it.

As the first anniversary approaches, something shifts. The year that was full of firsts begins to feel like something else - the lasts. The last time you heard their voice. The last conversation. The last ordinary day before everything changed. This is a different kind of grief, and it catches many people off guard.

There is also an expectation that tends to build as the first anniversary approaches - the sense that the hardest part is almost over. But the second year brings its own challenges, and the biggest one is often that expectation itself.

When it isn't easier - when the grief is still there, still real, still present - the letdown can be significant.

Think of it this way. Carrying something heavy is manageable for a short time. But hold that same weight for long enough, and the fatigue becomes its own problem, separate from the weight itself.

It's not that the grief has gotten heavier; it's that you become tired from carrying it. And in the second year, people are often tired in ways they didn't anticipate. Tired of being sad. Tired of still needing support. Tired of grief being the thing that defines them.

What is also true is that the first year, as hard as it is, is doing something, whether it feels that way or not. Every day that passes is a day you have navigated without them. The things that were once unimaginable become, slowly, part of a new reality. You stop reaching for your phone to call them quite as often - because you are, without even trying, adapting.

The first year is full of that kind of quiet work. It happens in the background, beneath all the hard days, whether you can feel it or not.

JOY AND ABSENCE

Life continues. And at some point - maybe in the first year, maybe years from now - good things will happen again.

Weddings. Babies. Graduations. Milestones. Moments that are supposed to be purely happy. And in the middle of them, the absence of the person you lost will be felt as sharply as it ever was.

This is one of the things people are least prepared for. Not the grief on the hard days – that makes sense. But the grief that shows up on the good ones.

What people discover is that joy and grief can exist at the same time. In the same moment, even. You can be genuinely happy and genuinely heartbroken simultaneously. You can be laughing and missing them in the same breath. We are used to feeling one thing at a time. Grief asks more of us than that.

But your conflicting emotions don't have to fight each other for space. You have room for all of it. You can move back and forth - honoring the happiness and honoring the loss - without either one having to cancel the other out.

Bittersweet is the word for it. And grief, more than almost anything else in life, teaches us what bittersweet really means.

WHAT HELPS

After everything that has been said in these pages, it would be easy to feel like grief is something that just happens to you - and in many ways it is. But there are things that help.

Not things that fix it or speed it up. But instead, some things that make it more bearable, one day at a time.

Research on grief is consistent about three things in particular:

1. Being around people who understand. Not everyone will. But finding even one or two people who get it – who don't need it explained, who aren't uncomfortable with your sadness, who can sit with you in it – makes a difference. This is why grief groups, formal or informal, tend to help in ways that even close friendships sometimes can't.

2. Talking about the person and to the person who died. Say their name. Tell stories. Keep them present in conversation. Many grievers worry about bringing them up - that it will make others uncomfortable, or that it means they aren't moving forward. The opposite tends to be true. Talking about them is not dwelling. It is just love, looking for someplace to go. And talking to them – in the car, in the quiet, wherever feels right - is something many grievers find surprisingly comforting. There is no wrong way to stay connected.

3. Having some structure in daily life. Not a full schedule or a set of goals. Just enough routine to give the day shape. Something to get up for. Something that moves you from one part of the day to the next. Grief is unpredictable by nature - a little structure provides some counterbalance to that.

Something you can count on, even when little else feels reliable. And when the big questions start crowding in - where will I live, how will I manage, how am I going to get through the rest of my life without them- try to reel it back. Those questions are real, and they will get answered. But they belong to a future version of you, one who will have more to work with than you do right now. The only place you have any real power is the present. Grief, more than almost any other experience, makes that clear.

A FINAL NOTE

The foundation of our work has always been the people we work with. Their honesty, their resilience, the way they give voice to things that are almost impossible to say out loud. We listen carefully, we honor what we hear, and it finds its way into everything we do.

Here is one such example. A story shared by a griever, that has stayed with us ever since:

A woman had strep throat one winter. Her husband, a paramedic, kept reminding her to drink fluids. Her throat hurt so badly she could barely speak. "I can't drink," she told him. "I can't even swallow." His response was simple: "Of course you can swallow. It just hurts."

Shortly after this incident, he died. And for a very long time, she struggled, and she suffered. She didn't think she could make it, she wasn't sure she could go on. And then she remembered that moment, came back to his words. And from that point on, any time she said to herself, "I can't do this," she heard him - of course you can, it just hurts.

Grief asks everything of you. Your patience, your energy, your routine, your identity, your relationships, your sense of the future - all of it has been touched by this. There will be times you want to give up. Times you will say I can't do this.

Let this be your reminder.

Of course you can. It just hurts.

THE GRIEF CONTINUES – BUT SO DOES THE SUPPORT

This book was about the first year. When you are ready for more, our GRIEF framework was built for exactly this. Every practical question you have - or will have - is in there.

G - Grounding. How do I sleep when I can't sleep? Why does it matter what I eat? How do I get myself out of bed and moving when everything feels pointless?

R - Rebuilding. How do I create a new routine? How do I function at work? How do I get through the day without falling apart?

I - Interacting. What do I say when someone asks "how are you?" How do I deal with family members who grieve differently? How do I handle the people who disappoint me?

E - Evolving. What do I do with the anger? The guilt? The resentment? How do I stop feeling so bad about myself? How do I find my way back to who I was?

F - Finding. What does my life look like now? How do I find motivation again? How do I figure out what comes next?

Grief is not something anyone knows how to do. There is no reason you should be expected to figure it out on your own. That is what we are here for.

ABOUT THE AUTHORS

Karyn Arnold was born in Belmar, New Jersey and raised in Bucks County, Pennsylvania, where she currently resides. She has a bachelor's degree in psychology and gerontology, along with her 200-hour CYTT and Reiki practitioner certification.

She has worked in the field of Grief and Loss for almost 25 years. In 2015, she created the website Grief in Common, an online community dedicated to connecting grievers based on background and similar circumstances of loss. Services include message boards, a live chat room, an online classroom, Zoom support groups, education programs, and individual support.

Karyn has worked with grievers worldwide and has encountered just about every grief and loss a person can experience. Her professional and personal experience with grief means she understands this process in ways that few people can, and through her daily work, she aims to provide education, validation, and support. Through a simple 3-part process, Karyn takes the griever from where they've been, to where they are now, and tries to help them answer the question, "Where do I go from here?"

Connect with Karyn: www.griefincommon.com

Kelly Daugherty, a seasoned social worker with over 25 years of clinical experience, is a Fellow in Thanatology: Death, Dying, and Bereavement. Anchored in Malta, New York, she owns Kelly Daugherty, LCSW, PLLC, and the Center for Informed Grief, LLC. Her commitment to grief and loss stems from her personal journey, which began with her mother's death from breast cancer during her teenage years. This significant loss led Kelly to volunteer with a Hospice Children's Bereavement program and set the foundation for her career. Every day, Kelly finds meaning in her grief by helping both individuals navigate the complexities of grief and professionals aiming to understand it better.

Determined to revolutionize how grief support is provided, Kelly offers a wealth of tools and insights to those grappling with the death of loved ones and to the professionals dedicated to helping them. The Center for Informed Grief aims to create a more grief-informed society by benefiting individuals, families, schools, and broader communities. Through comprehensive training for educators and therapists, consultation with schools, online courses, and active social media communities, Kelly ensures that nobody faces their grief journey in solitude.

In addition, Kelly is the lead author of *The Grief Experience: Tools for Acceptance, Resilience and Connection* and has contributed her expertise to *Holistic Mental Health, Volume 1*; *Brave Kids, Volumes 1, 2, and 3*; and *Ultimate Guide to Self Healing, Volume 6.*

Connect with Kelly: www.kellydaugherty.com

RESOURCES

www.griefladies.com
www.griefincommon
www.centerforinformedgrief.com

GRIEF *Ladies*

A Guide to What Comes Next

1 LISTEN TO THE PODCAST

The GRIEF Ladies: A Guide to What Comes Next is available on all major podcast platforms and YouTube. New episodes every week — real conversations about what grief actually looks like.

Spotify · Apple Podcasts · YouTube

2 EXPLORE OUR COURSES

Online workshops and grief programs built for grieving individuals — from the newly bereaved to those navigating life after significant loss.

Purchase at:
www.griefladies.com

3 JOIN THE COMMUNITY

The GRIEF Ladies Community on Facebook is a free group for people navigating grief. A place to feel less alone, and to be with others who understand.

Join at:
facebook.com/groups/griefladies

4 FIND RESOURCES

Journals, guided meditations, and community events — all designed to support you through grief, one step at a time.

www.griefladies.com

WWW.GRIEFLADIES.COM

Made in the USA
Coppell, TX
24 June 2026

83376871R00017